This Book Belongs to :

_____

_____

_____

A

Website
Username
Password
Notes

Website
Username
Password
Notes

Website
Username
Password
Notes

Website
Username
Password
Notes

A

Website
Username
Password
Notes

Website
Username
Password
Notes

Website
Username
Password
Notes

Website
Username
Password
Notes

A

Website
Username
Password
Notes

Website
Username
Password
Notes

Website
Username
Password
Notes

Website
Username
Password
Notes

A

Website
Username
Password
Notes

Website
Username
Password
Notes

Website
Username
Password
Notes

Website
Username
Password
Notes

B

Website
Username
Password
Notes

Website
Username
Password
Notes

Website
Username
Password
Notes

Website
Username
Password
Notes

B

Website
Username
Password
Notes

Website
Username
Password
Notes

Website
Username
Password
Notes

Website
Username
Password
Notes

B

Website
Username
Password
Notes

Website
Username
Password
Notes

Website
Username
Password
Notes

Website
Username
Password
Notes

B

| Website |
| Username |
| Password |
| Notes |

| Website |
| Username |
| Password |
| Notes |

| Website |
| Username |
| Password |
| Notes |

| Website |
| Username |
| Password |
| Notes |

C

Website
Username
Password
Notes

Website
Username
Password
Notes

Website
Username
Password
Notes

Website
Username
Password
Notes

C

- Website
- Username
- Password
- Notes

- Website
- Username
- Password
- Notes

- Website
- Username
- Password
- Notes

- Website
- Username
- Password
- Notes

C

Website
Username
Password
Notes

Website
Username
Password
Notes

Website
Username
Password
Notes

Website
Username
Password
Notes

C

Website
Username
Password
Notes

Website
Username
Password
Notes

Website
Username
Password
Notes

Website
Username
Password
Notes

D

Website
Username
Password
Notes

Website
Username
Password
Notes

Website
Username
Password
Notes

Website
Username
Password
Notes

D

- Website
- Username
- Password
- Notes

- Website
- Username
- Password
- Notes

- Website
- Username
- Password
- Notes

- Website
- Username
- Password
- Notes

D

Website
Username
Password
Notes

Website
Username
Password
Notes

Website
Username
Password
Notes

Website
Username
Password
Notes

D

Website
Username
Password
Notes

Website
Username
Password
Notes

Website
Username
Password
Notes

Website
Username
Password
Notes

E

Website
Username
Password
Notes

Website
Username
Password
Notes

Website
Username
Password
Notes

Website
Username
Password
Notes

E

- Website
- Username
- Password
- Notes

- Website
- Username
- Password
- Notes

- Website
- Username
- Password
- Notes

- Website
- Username
- Password
- Notes

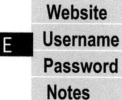

Website
Username
Password
Notes

Website
Username
Password
Notes

Website
Username
Password
Notes

Website
Username
Password
Notes

E

Website
Username
Password
Notes

Website
Username
Password
Notes

Website
Username
Password
Notes

Website
Username
Password
Notes

F

Website
Username
Password
Notes

Website
Username
Password
Notes

Website
Username
Password
Notes

Website
Username
Password
Notes

F

Website
Username
Password
Notes

Website
Username
Password
Notes

Website
Username
Password
Notes

Website
Username
Password
Notes

F

- Website
- Username
- Password
- Notes

- Website
- Username
- Password
- Notes

- Website
- Username
- Password
- Notes

- Website
- Username
- Password
- Notes

F

Website	
Username	
Password	
Notes	

Website	
Username	
Password	
Notes	

Website	
Username	
Password	
Notes	

Website	
Username	
Password	
Notes	

G

- Website
- Username
- Password
- Notes

- Website
- Username
- Password
- Notes

- Website
- Username
- Password
- Notes

- Website
- Username
- Password
- Notes

G

- Website
- Username
- Password
- Notes

- Website
- Username
- Password
- Notes

- Website
- Username
- Password
- Notes

- Website
- Username
- Password
- Notes

G

- Website
- Username
- Password
- Notes

- Website
- Username
- Password
- Notes

- Website
- Username
- Password
- Notes

- Website
- Username
- Password
- Notes

G

Website
Username
Password
Notes

Website
Username
Password
Notes

Website
Username
Password
Notes

Website
Username
Password
Notes

H

Website
Username
Password
Notes

Website
Username
Password
Notes

Website
Username
Password
Notes

Website
Username
Password
Notes

H

Website
Username
Password
Notes

Website
Username
Password
Notes

Website
Username
Password
Notes

Website
Username
Password
Notes

Website
Username
Password
Notes

H

Website
Username
Password
Notes

Website
Username
Password
Notes

Website
Username
Password
Notes

H

- **Website**
- **Username**
- **Password**
- **Notes**

- **Website**
- **Username**
- **Password**
- **Notes**

- **Website**
- **Username**
- **Password**
- **Notes**

- **Website**
- **Username**
- **Password**
- **Notes**

Website	
Username	
Password	
Notes	

Website	
Username	
Password	
Notes	

Website	
Username	
Password	
Notes	

Website	
Username	
Password	
Notes	

Website
Username
Password
Notes

Website
Username
Password
Notes

Website
Username
Password
Notes

Website
Username
Password
Notes

Website
Username
Password
Notes

Website
Username
Password
Notes

Website
Username
Password
Notes

Website
Username
Password
Notes

Website
Username
Password
Notes

Website
Username
Password
Notes

Website
Username
Password
Notes

Website
Username
Password
Notes

| Website |
| Username |
| Password |
| Notes |

J
| Website |
| Username |
| Password |
| Notes |

| Website |
| Username |
| Password |
| Notes |

| Website |
| Username |
| Password |
| Notes |

J

Website
Username
Password
Notes

Website
Username
Password
Notes

Website
Username
Password
Notes

Website
Username
Password
Notes

Website	
Username	
Password	
Notes	

J	Website	
	Username	
	Password	
	Notes	

Website	
Username	
Password	
Notes	

Website	
Username	
Password	
Notes	

J

Website
Username
Password
Notes

Website
Username
Password
Notes

Website
Username
Password
Notes

Website
Username
Password
Notes

Website
Username
Password
Notes

K
Website
Username
Password
Notes

Website
Username
Password
Notes

Website
Username
Password
Notes

K

Website
Username
Password
Notes

Website
Username
Password
Notes

Website
Username
Password
Notes

Website
Username
Password
Notes

K

Website	
Username	
Password	
Notes	

Website	
Username	
Password	
Notes	

Website	
Username	
Password	
Notes	

Website	
Username	
Password	
Notes	

K

Website
Username
Password
Notes

Website
Username
Password
Notes

Website
Username
Password
Notes

Website
Username
Password
Notes

L

| Website |
| Username |
| Password |
| Notes |

| Website |
| Username |
| Password |
| Notes |

| Website |
| Username |
| Password |
| Notes |

| Website |
| Username |
| Password |
| Notes |

L

- Website
- Username
- Password
- Notes

- Website
- Username
- Password
- Notes

- Website
- Username
- Password
- Notes

- Website
- Username
- Password
- Notes

L

| Website |
| Username |
| Password |
| Notes |

| Website |
| Username |
| Password |
| Notes |

| Website |
| Username |
| Password |
| Notes |

| Website |
| Username |
| Password |
| Notes |

L

Website
Username
Password
Notes

Website
Username
Password
Notes

Website
Username
Password
Notes

Website
Username
Password
Notes

Website
Username
Password
Notes

Website
Username
Password
M **Notes**

Website
Username
Password
Notes

Website
Username
Password
Notes

Website
Username
Password
Notes

Website
Username
Password
Notes

M

Website
Username
Password
Notes

Website
Username
Password
Notes

M

Website
Username
Password
Notes

Website
Username
Password
Notes

Website
Username
Password
Notes

Website
Username
Password
Notes

Website
Username
Password
Notes

Website
Username
Password
Notes

M

Website
Username
Password
Notes

Website
Username
Password
Notes

N

| Website |
| Username |
| Password |
| Notes |

| Website |
| Username |
| Password |
| Notes |

| Website |
| Username |
| Password |
| Notes |

| Website |
| Username |
| Password |
| Notes |

Website
Username
Password
Notes

Website
Username
Password
Notes

N

Website
Username
Password
Notes

Website
Username
Password
Notes

N

Website
Username
Password
Notes

Website
Username
Password
Notes

Website
Username
Password
Notes

Website
Username
Password
Notes

Website
Username
Password
Notes

Website
Username
Password
Notes

N

Website
Username
Password
Notes

Website
Username
Password
Notes

Website
Username
Password
Notes

Website
Username
Password
Notes

O

Website
Username
Password
Notes

Website
Username
Password
Notes

O

Website
Username
Password
Notes

Website
Username
Password
Notes

Website
Username
Password
Notes

Website
Username
Password
Notes

Website
Username
Password
Notes

Website
Username
Password
Notes

O

Website
Username
Password
Notes

Website
Username
Password
Notes

Website
Username
Password
Notes

Website
Username
Password
Notes

O

Website
Username
Password
Notes

Website
Username
Password
Notes

Website
Username
Password
Notes

Website
Username
Password
Notes

P

Website
Username
Password
Notes

Website
Username
Password
Notes

P

Website
Username
Password
Notes

Website
Username
Password
Notes

Website
Username
Password
Notes

Website
Username
Password
Notes

Website
Username
Password
Notes

Website
Username
Password
Notes

P

Website
Username
Password
Notes

Website
Username
Password
Notes

Website
Username
Password
Notes

Website
Username
Password
Notes

P

Website
Username
Password
Notes

Website
Username
Password
Notes

Website
Username
Password
Notes

Website
Username
Password
Notes

Q
Website
Username
Password
Notes

Website
Username
Password
Notes

Website
Username
Password
Notes

Website
Username
Password
Notes

Q

Website
Username
Password
Notes

Website
Username
Password
Notes

Website
Username
Password
Notes

Website
Username
Password
Notes

Q
Website
Username
Password
Notes

Website
Username
Password
Notes

Website	
Username	
Password	
Notes	

Website	
Username	
Password	
Notes	

Q

Website	
Username	
Password	
Notes	

Website	
Username	
Password	
Notes	

Website	
Username	
Password	
Notes	

Website	
Username	
Password	
Notes	

R

Website	
Username	
Password	
Notes	

Website	
Username	
Password	
Notes	

Website
Username
Password
Notes

Website
Username
Password
Notes

Website
Username
Password
Notes

R

Website
Username
Password
Notes

Website
Username
Password
Notes

Website
Username
Password
Notes

R
Website
Username
Password
Notes

Website
Username
Password
Notes

R

Website
Username
Password
Notes

Website
Username
Password
Notes

Website
Username
Password
Notes

Website
Username
Password
Notes

Website
Username
Password
Notes

Website
Username
Password
Notes

S
Website
Username
Password
Notes

Website
Username
Password
Notes

Website
Username
Password
Notes

Website
Username
Password
Notes

Website
Username
Password
Notes

S

Website
Username
Password
Notes

Website
Username
Password
Notes

Website
Username
Password
Notes

S
Website
Username
Password
Notes

Website
Username
Password
Notes

Website
Username
Password
Notes

Website
Username
Password
Notes

Website
Username
Password
Notes

S

Website
Username
Password
Notes

Website
Username
Password
Notes

Website
Username
Password
Notes

Website
Username
T **Password**
Notes

Website
Username
Password
Notes

Website
Username
Password
Notes

Website
Username
Password
Notes

Website
Username
Password
Notes

T

Website
Username
Password
Notes

T

- Website
- Username
- Password
- Notes

- Website
- Username
- Password
- Notes

- Website
- Username
- Password
- Notes

- Website
- Username
- Password
- Notes

Website
Username
Password
Notes

Website
Username
Password
Notes

Website
Username
Password
Notes

T

Website
Username
Password
Notes

Website
Username
Password
Notes

Website
Username
Password
Notes

Website
Username
Password
Notes

Website
Username
Password
Notes

Website
Username
Password
Notes

Website
Username
Password
Notes

Website
Username
Password
Notes

U

Website
Username
Password
Notes

Website
Username
Password
Notes

Website
Username
Password
Notes

Website
Username
Password
U **Notes**

Website
Username
Password
Notes

Website
Username
Password
Notes

Website
Username
Password
Notes

Website
Username
Password
Notes

U

Website
Username
Password
Notes

Website
Username
Password
Notes

Website
Username
Password
Notes

Website
Username
Password
Notes

Website
Username
Password
Notes

Website
Username
Password
Notes

Website
Username
Password
Notes

Website
Username
Password
Notes

V

Website
Username
Password
Notes

Website
Username
Password
Notes

Website
Username
Password
Notes

Website
Username
Password
Notes

Website
Username
Password
Notes

Website
Username
Password
Notes

Website
Username
Password
Notes

Website
Username
Password
Notes

V

Website
Username
Password
Notes

Website
Username
Password
Notes

Website
Username
Password
Notes

Website
Username
Password
Notes

Website
Username
Password
Notes

Website
Username
Password
Notes

Website
Username
Password
Notes

Website
Username
Password
Notes

W

Website
Username
Password
Notes

Website
Username
Password
Notes

Website
Username
Password
Notes

Website
Username
Password
Notes

W

Website
Username
Password
Notes

Website
Username
Password
Notes

Website
Username
Password
Notes

Website
Username
Password
Notes

W

Website
Username
Password
Notes

Website
Username
Password
Notes

Website
Username
Password
Notes

Website
Username
Password
Notes

X
Website
Username
Password
Notes

Website
Username
Password
Notes

Website
Username
Password
Notes

Website
Username
Password
Notes

X

Website
Username
Password
Notes

Website
Username
Password
Notes

Website
Username
Password
Notes

Website
Username
Password
Notes

X

Website
Username
Password
Notes

Website
Username
Password
Notes

Website
Username
Password
Notes

Website
Username
Password
Notes

X

Website
Username
Password
Notes

Website
Username
Password
Notes

Website
Username
Password
Notes

Website
Username
Password
Notes

Y
Website
Username
Password
Notes

Website
Username
Password
Notes

Website
Username
Password
Notes

Website
Username
Password
Notes

Website
Username
Password
Notes

Y

Website
Username
Password
Notes

Website
Username
Password
Notes

Website
Username
Password
Notes

Y
Website
Username
Password
Notes

Website
Username
Password
Notes

Website
Username
Password
Notes

Website
Username
Password
Notes

Website
Username
Password
Notes

Y

Website
Username
Password
Notes

Website
Username
Password
Notes

Website
Username
Password
Notes

Z
Website
Username
Password
Notes

Website
Username
Password
Notes

Website
Username
Password
Notes

Website
Username
Password
Notes

Website
Username
Password
Notes

Z

| Website |
| Username |
| Password |
| Notes |

| Website |
| Username |
| Password |
| Notes |

| Website |
| Username |
| Password |
| Notes |

Z

| Website |
| Username |
| Password |
| Notes |

Website
Username
Password
Notes

Website
Username
Password
Notes

Website
Username
Password
Notes

Website
Username
Password
Notes

Z

Notes

Notes

Notes

Notes

www.ingramcontent.com/pod-product-compliance
Lightning Source LLC
LaVergne TN
LVHW021601080125
800829LV00009B/613